MASAHIRO KASUYA

The Beginning of the World

Abingdon/Nashville

In the beginning everything was very dark.

Then God said, "Let the heavens be bright!"
And he created the light.

And he called the light day and the darkness night.
So it became morning, and the first day began.

And God rolled up the heavens like a big blue cloth

and made the water that falls from the sky and the water on the earth.
This happened on the second day.

Then God let the water flow from the earth.
The land became dry.

And God let grass, herbs, and trees grow on the earth.
This happened on the third day.

And God put the sun into the sky,
that it may shine during the day.

But for the night he created the moon and stars.
This happened on the fourth day.

And God filled the water with many swimming animals.

Large and small fish swam around in the sea.

God let the birds fly in the air.

This happened on the fifth day.

And God created the animals of the earth.

Some grew very big.

At last God created man and woman and gave them a beautiful garden.

There they lived with the animals. This happened on the sixth day.

On the seventh day God rested from all his creations.

God's day of rest became the Sabbath for the people.

Many thousands of years passed. The people multiplied

all over the world and built themselves houses.

New people are being born everyday,

and God gives each person a special face—yours too.

THE BEGINNING OF THE WORLD

ISBN 0-687-02765-9